Volume 73 of the Yale Series of Younger Poets

BIN
RAMKE The
Difference
between Night
and Day

Foreword by Richard Hugo

New Haven and London   Yale University Press   1978

Published with assistance from
The Mary Cady Tew Memorial Fund.

Designed by Sally Harris.
Set in Monotype Janson type
by Michael & Winifred Bixler, Boston, Massachusetts.
Printed in the United States of America by
The Alpine Press, South Braintree, Massachusetts.

Published in Great Britain, Europe, Africa, and
Asia (except Japan) by Yale University Press,
Ltd., London. Distributed in Latin America by
Kaiman & Polon, Inc., New York City; in
Australia and New Zealand by Book & Film
Services, Artarmon, N.S.W., Australia; and in
Japan by Harper & Row, Publishers, Tokyo Office.

Library of Congress Cataloging in Publication Data

Ramke, Bin, 1947–
    The difference between night and day.

    (The Yale series of younger poets ; v. 73)
    I. Title. II. Series.
PS3568.A446D5 1978   811'.5'4   77–16790
ISBN 0-300-02225-5
ISBN 0-300-02232-8 pbk.

for Stanley Plumly

Contents

IV

Foreword

An old theory, by now a cliché, has it that artists are nobodies when not practicing their art. Most often this is applied to actors. The bright star on the stage becomes a drab blob the moment the play is over, and starts to sparkle again the next evening when the curtain rises.

Reading "The Difference between Night and Day" I'm reminded of this theory, not because I suspect Ramke is a blob of any sort, but because his poems are so honestly rooted in isolation that they suggest a man with no way of reaching others except through his writing. The gains are made and the losses counted in isolation. When Ramke is writing he has no friends. Isolation is a somewhat shopworn theme in modern poetry, but when it is this deeply felt, this personal, it becomes new. New because it functions dynamically in poems that are new and unusual.

Not so unusual that no ancestors hover in the background. One of Ramke's ancestors is Wallace Stevens, and like Stevens, Ramke risks an apparent coldness. What happens around him seems to run a poor second to his fantasy life, and in the early parts of this book we often get a picture of one for whom caring does not carry high priority and to whom escape from feeling is essential to survival. Yet if I believed Ramke a cold poet I would not have picked him to be the winner of the Yale Series of Younger Poets. Ramke's coldness is not a lack of passion, but the coldness of the void the imagination must inhabit to receive the disparate events, both internal and external, the gradations of response to those events, the mysteries of things—those "strange birds" that "call, hidden in the sky." What we feel is the isolation he must feel to write the poems.

Paradoxically, and again like Stevens, one of Ramke's assets is his generosity. A good poem is usually generous, but there are degrees. Many poets stick to one small part of their natures because that is where they find the poems. Hunting for words seems confined to a limited area set aside by the psyche for that purpose. Other sides of self are excluded because to operate at all the imagination senses it must restrict the size of its base of operations. For such poets, generosity usually takes the form of a tune played well for us, a stance struck convincingly that we welcome for the duration of the poem.

Ramke's generosity is rarer. He goes to more parts of self than do most poets, and what we receive is not simply a tune played well (though that too) or a stance convincingly held, but an open invitation to experience as much of the poet's total sensibility as he can locate. It takes an imagination gifted in special ways to create good poems out of the diffuse worlds we carry inside. Bin Ramke's imagination has those special gifts.

In this collection, Ramke is suspended between two extremes, one earthly, the other astral. One in day. The other at night. One he must live in. The other he must escape to. As the book unfolds more and more the poems arrive intact from the first world, the earthly. No poems come complete from the second world, the astral. The poems must return to earth to find stability, and Ramke needs daylight to see what he's doing. Anyway, words are found on earth.

Early in the book the earthly world is characterized by restricted numbers of possibilities. In the title poem, seven lines are about day, the other twenty-six about night. On earth things must be themselves before they become something else. The astral world luxuriates in metaphor. The "fish" that "move like stars in the dark ocean" don't exist during day. They are not real fish—"Nothing like them under the sun."

Night, the astral world, offers vast possibilities. That is one of its prime attractions for the poet. At night the speaker can welcome his isolation—"live in a copper dome"—can take "snapshots of God," who appears in the form of stars. Role switching comes easy. Any mask will do. Astronomers, not ichthyologists, are the fish experts. And at night the poet can find a fish (a failed self) far from its natural home, dead in its attempt to find a new one, the ideal home. The poet can pocket the fish and go on searching for love. At night personal failure can be put away or redeemed, and the search for the ideal, "clean" self continued.

At night the poet can contemplate and accept "how useless" he is, how inept—"I have charts but cannot read them." But faith can be maintained in the astral setting, and the poet pose as the expert (the astronomers get away with it), stating facts that cannot be proven and must be taken on faith:

> I tell you a star is green
> but you cannot see it.

He can feign wisdom in the role of prophet:

> I predict the end of your sun
> in twelve million years.

Despite the opportunities presented by night and his willingness to take advantage and project both pitiful and grandiose roles, what he knows for sure appears in the immediate earthly terms of crime, biology, and mortality:

> There is murder in the sky
> like tossed bones
> and counted teeth . . .

Back on earth in daylight we find the geometric "planes and cones that pop and glisten," as well as the "ugly fish" who in death are denied the final dignity of "properly" closed eyes. Propriety would not be a consideration among the stars. The duality of the earthly world, the attractive and the unattractive, is on a scale too easily understood, too real and defined and final for the imagination's ambition. The poem ends both firmly and wistfully:

> The stars in the desert are a dream of fish.

A starry world of expansive metaphor and extreme possibilities is a dream of Ramke's.

A critic who would illuminate Ramke's work by studying both the work and the poet's life would probably take more than casual note of the poem "The Feast of the Body of Christ in Texas." The poet is forced to take part in a three-hour march of Roman Catholics, a small minority within the community, through the streets of his Texas home town "under the eyes of the Baptists." The angel who "sat in our one peach tree" is gone when they return and the poet, twelve years old by my mathematics, begins to develop personal escape routes now that the chances of heavenly redemption seem remote. There are cities to go to, Chicago, Los Angeles, or a smaller town, Biloxi, which, I think I remember, enjoyed a reputation as Sin Center around 1959, and "a thousand Omahas." Already the poet has begun to compound reality, to create a world of other possibilities he can escape to.

Then Venice, where he imagines himself a child, and a message that tries to be comforting written across his ceiling by a trick of light. But for now he finds comfort in the immediate hedonistic devouring of peaches and in a discussion of the horse dung just now deposited outside the dining-room window. Once again, the limited duality of mundane existence. The astral world of expanded chances that would replace the glamorous cities is not yet available for his imagination to explore.

In the first poem, Ramke told us "nothing is clean but war and music," and throughout the book we find wars being fought or recalled. Often war is necessary to locate the music. The music is always necessary to fight the war. But the wars Ramke fights become more and more local as the book unfolds, and by the final section they are fought here on earth, inside the earthbound protagonist who sometimes is Ramke and other times seems a fictional character. And what are the spoils left to the victor? Abatement of guilt? Self-forgiveness? Paling of regret? A basis for self-love? Those surely, but also words.

To win a war we must accept the sad selves we become during hostilities. As Ramke puts it in "Biography of a Strangler,"

> . . . since nothing
>
> comes home alive from the dark wood
> of Europe, you cannot choose
> whom you love. This is the story
> of one man's long life.

And again, by the end of the book, while this sense of isolation in a world where choice is impossible is still strong, the world itself is reduced to the local and immediate.

> You cannot choose
> whom you love
> on the way to Chicago.

Our chances of finding a worthy love are still poor. But now this is not a principle of existence, only the end result of limited circumstances.

Solitude, finally, is not only lovely, it is the only place we can go to escape the uniform degradation of our lives. And the isolation each feels is not the enemy as defined by the social scientists but the hero of our survival. According to "Entropy," a unique poem, that "we" is doomed. The "I" can make enormous gains in isolation, and the "he" that survives survives by using the gains of the "I" to convert the losses of the "we," our losses, to something wholesome and sustaining. The poem is a microcosm of the whole book.

More than Ramke's poignant momentary acceptances of his life, and, by implication, ours, more than his tentative messages which no matter how wise are offered in humility, more than his graceful quick journeys back and forth between the earthly world of limited possibilities and the high starry void where he hopes, as only a child can, to find some ideal "clean" self, and more than his eventual coming to terms with his limited existence only to find it is not so limited after all, it is his imagination I find exciting. He can't be anticipated and his moves, no matter how unexpected, seem right, not some vain pose that plays to the audience for a gasp of surprise.

Ramke's words often seem touched by magic: they let us know, in some subtle way that must be connected to music, that they are saying more than they seem to be, and we are intrigued into wanting to locate and understand that something else.

That something else may turn out to be ourselves, the wars we fight, social, sexual, or religious, the childlike journeys we made and, if lucky, still make to the stars, and the triumphant veterans we are in the wide eye of hard won words.

Richard Hugo

Acknowledgments

Acknowledgment is made to the following publications for poems that originally appeared in them.

American Review: "*Confessio Amantis:* For Frederick Rolfe, Baron Corvo"

Barataria Review: "Biography of a Strangler"

The Georgia Review: "The Channel Swimmer," "Martyrdom: A Love Poem"

The Iowa Review: "The Difference between Night and Day"

The Ohio Review: "Appalling Light," "The Feast of the Body of Christ in Texas," "A History of the West," "Living Near Any Ocean: Insomnia and Guilt," "A Nod toward True Love and Fidelity"

Outerbridge: "The Movement of Birds like Years"

Poetry: "Secrets of the Saints: First Glimmerings"

Shenandoah: "Entropy"

The Southern Review: "The Husband's Guilt," "Lines of Blood," "Poems for a Tall, Sad Lady"

I

And emptiness is greatest where man
was rather than where he was not.
Interstellar space is not empty, but
there is no worse emptiness than a
house in ruins.

—Miroslav Holub

Living Near Any Ocean:
Insomnia and Guilt

1

A bit of the sea sounds delicately in one ear
when you cannot go to sleep; you wish
you were home and the noise were Bach, Brandenburg,
perhaps, in B-flat major. The moon
never changed anything and yet
the problem would not be the same
if the walls were dark and the last petal
of a nameless flower in a crystal vase
did not glow so delicately:
few secrets lie so quiet for so long.

2

If pardon were possible, if it were,
it would come at night under a partial moon
on a beach white as bone, cold;
nothing under the world's sun gleams
more elegant than a jet plane,
a machine long and lean-boned
like razors fitted in a velvet case:
nothing is clean but war and music.

3

Fragile-faced women upstairs
in the dark bear your children: listen
carefully, and if the waves
will for a moment lie still
you will hear their small scream.

The bones of the ear are unbelievably
small and can never be mended.

4

Bach on the battlefield, blood,
and the alliteration of bees chase
from the hives the honey-robbers:
all this far from the ocean, far
from the pulse of large water.

5

It was thought bees were pure
in sex, sexless, made babies
of wax and nectar like tiny Galateas.

From the large pipes of the organ
in a ruined church a swarm of bees flew
driven mad by Bach. I watched this
during the last war. I stood
on the coast. A storm threatened
and I was far from home and tired.

6

You will tell your wife
only some of the stories of war
and how it sounded
and what you did during the night.
At times a cup of coffee meant more than love,
though you had women across your bed
like captured pennants, like dirty shirts.

Entropy

Some of the evil of my tale
may have been inherent in our
circumstances.
—*T. E. Lawrence*

1

Vast petals of poppy burn
a brilliant hole in landscape:
the land lies riddled with heat.
The murders our evening paper tells
are not those we each commit
under this stress of heat.
Among our flowers butterflies
tatter their flimsy lives. Pray
for the drowning city,
but for the city consumed by heat
listen to the scatter
of its dry seed.

2

The formidable memory of birds
brings them back by millions
each summer. For two days
the sky darkens beneath their wings,
their call is that faint language
a citizen barely recalls:
a thin, scattered remembrance
of an age of flight.

And we become a city of lizards
flat against the burning rocks
hanging our shriveled sex in bundles
like garlic from the rafters,
an amulet against dark dangers.

We fear what comes with the cool of evening,
we are terrified of night.

3

And we fear such things as great success
or obvious failure. We know ourselves.
Each house in our terrible town has a garden,
a wall, and a secret. We breed garish flowers
to tend with cruel care.
We are small and all very much alike.

In our city if you need a place to sleep
knock on any door. If it opens, the smell
of fear will drive you back into the street.

Let us consider that our fear is a large black bird—
this is hypothesis—and this bird's solemn
wing beat marks a cycle of months, perhaps years.
In our beds at night we breathe longer breaths
to keep time with our peculiar fate.
We go slowly through the day, we try to be part
of what we do not understand. I have kept
our secret but told you of our fear.

4

Wrapped in yourself speak
to us as a prophet should, fresh
from the desert. Tell us the story
of stones and small immortal snakes,
the story of long effulgent time.

5

On the first of July, 1961, Louis-Ferdinand Céline
spoke in our Municipal Auditorium. The speech

was called "Life Comes to You in the Morning."
I shall not be great in my own language, he said,
I am one who grows in translation.
There was much applause, then a clown show followed.

The speech lasted twelve hours. We heard
the purr of bees, the brittle crash of fountains,
voices in the distance rising and falling
like flocks of birds. We saw the spittle
dry on his lips. He spoke
one long single breath, and at the end
only I was left to hear.

I alone applauded, till my hands bled;
I threw the poppies to his feet;
I alone saw the clowns
perform unspeakable acts
upon each other.
Later, the speaker and the clowns gone,
I watched the spiders
weave stars in the rafters.

6

A man drives his car in the desert.
He is alone. Our city lights the sky
in a small corner of his horizon.
Soon he will sleep, or die, and dream
of acres and acres of poppies
with butterflies skimming their surface
and a few magnificent spiders
drifting on threads,
riding the waves of heat.

Secrets of the Saints

First Glimmerings

An old sea festers on the beach,
Rorschach in starlight,
fundamental, inevitable, cold.

Someone travels to the stars as to
the movies to see what's playing.
I find it difficult to stand
on this single earth. A hurricane
could clean its face, spew
its salty punctuation along
the lines of beach. Women

are probably no better than men:
my sisters, too, look long
out the window, stare
at the filling flesh of beach,
feel a new tide, a tremor of night.

Death of a Dog

The wearing of time on the wrist
reveals the modern soul: once
it was kept in a pocket
somewhere near the liver; some
still hang it from a chain
around the neck symbolically.

At Touro Infirmary the Mexicans
always pay cash. One couple
for three years paid every week
on the death of their child
born premature, killed by time
or its absence. In the modern mode
this is called a time-payment.

Whatever else hangs in the summer air
around those front steps ticks
silently but strong, like humidity
in New Orleans in June. I held
other jobs in that city, but none
that made me miss so much my dog
whose heart one day was not sufficient
unto the troubles thereof.

He loved me like clockwork while he lived.

Prodigal Son

Father, I watched myself make coffee this morning
while leaning against the kitchen sink,
back bowed just past an esthetic
degree to bear the weight of morning.
Arms folded, I watched the boiling water drip.

I have too little to say. I left you
while taking my portion: a bad back,
a too quick eye for women's breasts,
a passion for bad food and good music,
a way of speaking on the telephone
that cost me two jobs already.

I have eaten those pods that I cast
before swine; I have sinned with boys
and women. I have no ambitions
that are not yours; I have exchanged
for a mess of pottage my mirror—
when I looked in its boiling face
all I saw was you.

Than to Burn

"You're cold" you say, and so I am:
the film took longer than expected,
the rain came sooner.

A man and his wife go to the movies like life
to see what they can see. The rain starts
down as if it mattered; we laugh

going home. Enough for now,
life asks so little, really, just that you keep
moving, please, don't hold up the line:

but there is the moon above us, beyond
rain and whatever else falls
on our shoulders as we pitch

through the streets to what,
knowing no better, we call home.
The moon shines through phosphorescent,

trickles down our necks
trivial as love, like light from streetlamps,
accompanies our small way home.

We are small and frightened
in such submarine light.
What we need is a system:

Rain,
how to get out
of the.

It has nothing to do with knowledge,
contrary to popular belief,
it cannot be taught.

Two Versions of History

1. For My Daughter

I look out the window and think
Arizona, the Depression is over.
My daughter says *this is too much.*

I look out a window and say California,
1945, the factories still tooled
for war. *This is too much.*

Well, then, I look out a window and say
Arkansas, late spring, the birds
have more to do than wait for us.

Too much. I lean out a window
and remember Texas, 1953, the bomb
will be here any moment,

I am six years old
and afraid of fallout, we do not have
shelter. I have never seen snow.

My daughter says *this is enough.*
Sometimes we needn't tell
all the secrets.

2. From My Daughter

Thirty years ago in Texas
he began his long life
curved like parentheses
inside a lady.
I am not old enough to know
but it is true.
There are other stories
in his night and I know them
all. I know them all.

A Nod toward True Love and Fidelity

She said: There is more to life than this, move
your hand and let me up. I did, kicked
the wet sheets off and stumped to the bathroom
to brush my gnashing teeth. I am not a violent
man, except when cleaning myself in the light
of a chaste morning.

Last night she said: You think about it too much,
it will make you sick. Years ago my father said:
What will your mother say?

And what they said is true, my hands are hairy
as my father's chest and lust seeps
into the air where I walk, all the people passing
in this small town turn and cover
the noses of the children.

I bow my head: I am a man of passion, guilty
as the day is long, guiltier—this turgid guilt
is more like night, dark and wet and warm
in the breezes of remembered childhood.
There is more to this than life:
in the kitchen I eat figs for breakfast,
strange birds call, hidden in the sky.

The Feast of the Body of Christ in Texas

An angel sat in our one peach tree
Corpus Christi morning
June, 1959.
He waited for us while we,
like a chosen people, walked
under the eyes of Baptists
through the streets of Beaumont
which the protestant cops
roped off for us.
It was only once a year
but we were very few and scared.

We walked three hours, sidewalks
squirmed beneath us in the heat.
What old world did we preserve?
What did we think
we were doing? When we returned
the angel was gone.

That night as heat rose in the room
I stood on the bed and looked
at Texas, across the fields at the glow
in orange, the plastic apotheosis,
the flatness of the land and
the effulgence of architecture.
From my room the view
of Howard Johnson's at the overpass
embraced all night travelers:
I pictured fragrant cities, Chicago,
Los Angeles, Biloxi, a thousand Omahas.

I will one day be a child
in Venice *a lume spento* in my room

with the light of St. Mark's spread
across the ceiling as pilgrims shuffle
in wet procession across flat stones.
The light will flicker as if trying
to become a sad dream and write
across my ceiling: Forget,
you are only a child.

But that Monday morning I had peaches
for breakfast. They were sweet
as sin on Sunday. A pile
of manure steamed outside
under the dining room window.
The horse had just turned the corner.
We discussed it. What else
would you suggest? Our fields
were full of horses, our mouths
full of peaches. We had walked
too many miles the day before
through the hostile town. The taste
of peaches was better than sex,
even, and the angel
never returned to Texas.

The Channel Swimmer

Blackberry tangled into traps, wild rose,
a mad dream of kudzu, and passionflower's
incessant vine all surround his old age
like last living relatives.

Let us pretend that we are old
and memorize our lives. I saw
my father watch his father
stand to say he was going home;
he stood in the house he had made
fifty years before; he stood
and remembered his father's house
whose ceilings and tall walls burned
in 1922. At first we tried to tell him
who and where he was, then let him go
with sad eyes and a dog:

he stood for an hour on the green hill
(we watched from the window):
for an hour he stood
while the dog slept.
When he turned we saw his face
and had he spoken he would have said:
The world is over. You may be children
but I do not know you. I
had a father. Tomorrow
I will try again. I had brothers
whom I taught to swim. You
will learn nothing from me.

Summer 1956: Louisiana

1

That land, dark and steeped in strange water,
full of night sounds at noon, flowed
into itself like dream, took us.
My elders sat rocking for days
discussing mosquitoes. I spoke
when spoken to.

I learned to make a kind
of limp fan from palmetto frond,
the palmate sheet of leaf
stripped with a knife to attached
slivers then dried.

Then children, too, could sit
and waft mosquitoes
leisurely away. Nights
were cool under trees. I remember
talk. Talk and food. And mosquitoes.

2

All day the sun directly above us
bleaches the sky as we talk,
waiting for night,
while the slack bayou erodes
its banks, widens
through the day. You
can see it glitter
above the mud which smooths
its slow journey.

What happens in this state is always memory
even before it happens. The mosquitoes lift
like fog and someone mentions the fire,
which we can barely see across the bayou
and through the trees, as if Sherman did it
a hundred years ago. It is not our fire,
and anyway, it cannot spread from the island.

An aunt brings iced tea,
the glasses bead sympathetically,
the children make designs
on the tables: circles, half-moons,
letters like *M* or *B*. The elders
talk of old war and mosquitoes.

After lunch some stay in the house—
do not ask what they do
in the locked rooms by twos. Perhaps
they make new memories, something
to discuss after supper. We walk

in the swamp to find snakes.
My brother finds the skull
and scattered bones of calf,
its eye filled with slick mud,
the brain packed neatly;
I see a pelvis like
a butterfly.

We imagine its small agony, make it
worse than what it could have been.
One of us thinks about dying.
My older brother carries
a rifle, though neither of us
is allowed to shoot.

We return to an uncle sweating
a new skin, an aunt drying dishes.
They ask us what we found.
They sound happy.

3

Twenty years later I still
cannot make what they did
behind those doors. No,
it was more than what you think—
history shone through
their eyes, though
they did not discuss it
at supper.

I have made my memories
but that water
still glistens, and somewhere
mosquitoes
have drops of my old blood:
we are all
such beasts under the skin.

And the skin sweats
like a tea glass at noon,
though I now live
north of the swamps
but south of the snow.

II

To say I love you is a humiliation.
    —Mona Van Duyn

The Difference between Night and Day

The geography of dream is complex
so I look to the stars, I live
within a copper dome taking snapshots
of God. He is ugly, he burns
red and orange. He has names like Aldebaran
and Alpha Centauri, ugly as he.
But he is clean.
Astronomers know the texture of fish,
and how it shines in the moonlight,
and how fish move like stars in the dark
ocean, that they are clean.
Nothing like them under the sun.

I pick up a fish dead in the road
at three in the morning in the desert.
I put it in my pocket
and continue to look for love in the night.

If you watch the tracks of the stars
you will see how useless I am.
I have charts but cannot read them.
I tell you a star is green
but you cannot see it.
I predict the end of your sun
in twelve million years.

There is murder in the sky
like tossed bones
and counted teeth;

like water in which we breathe
the air shines planes and cones
that pop and glisten.
The fish grow ugly in heat,
mouths puff open, eyes
will not close properly.
The stars in the desert are a dream of fish.

Lines of Blood

They used to tell us,
our aunts in black and starched
white collars,
that better than the mouth
the blood will tell
like a wolf in sheep-suit:
the man born wrong
hasn't the chance of a Chinaman.

I know the Chinese
whose blood sings a higher pitch,
nasal, where nosebleeds
are serious concerns:
the French know, too.
Native blood.

And take
Aunt Elise, born in Stuttgart
lived fifty years in El Paso.
Blood told

so during the war
they locked her up.
A good thing, too. German
blood is thick and turns
hard for lack of use.

And the Colonel back home
in Atlanta, when the hospital
mislabeled the bottle
and they gave him his houseboy's—
but you have heard that one.

There are so many stories
the blood can tell, its infusion
more poetry than all the breath
blown through the woods
to whistle under bushes
while the white stars listen.

A History of the West

1

Let us consider this phenomenon of Wife,
secret and common, like the white roots
of a sweet potato in a Mason jar,

like the dark underside of a kitchen sink.

2

Wife is like a new notebook:
with use it scrawls, blots,
wrinkles where the coffee spills,

or it keeps pure and empty.
In any case neither
should be read in strong light.

3

The happy husband lives always five years before.

4

I see Greek islands
hanging from threads of sunlight,
the sea too blue
for buoyancy

and figures in black
with faintly female faces
hidden as a wrinkled uterus
under coarse hooding lips.

Then Greece is a paradise
of boys
and Wife is like sails moving
against a setting sun,
black no matter what color.

5

A girl with brown hair
growing old in Ohio
looks through a window

doesn't notice three houses,
the barking dogs
or the rain:
she is in her kitchen,
the dishes are done.

6

A wife hears vague rumors
of life in Arizona.

She prepares a headache,
husband waits;

all life flickers
male and female in the sky.

A train passes,
the squeaks between boxcars

hint to them both
strongly of children.

7

Every son gleams
savagely through thickets
spying on his own dreams

wearing boots to bed.

A daughter's face,
a luminous dial,
tells time in the dark.

Guilt and the Long Ride Home

Stars swirl,
like a cigarette pitched
onto the night highway

seen through the rearview mirror;
or stars simmer
translucent as onion

sautéed in a black iron pot;
and other mnemic consequences
of the history

of a sly world's sleep.
Whatever is above
is untouchable

and leaves us laughing.
Notice how an umbrella,
old enough and black,

resembles a planetarium
which resembles in turn
the same sky

which you drive home
under, returning
to a small frail

wife after the assignation
begun during the romantic
rain, your one friend;

and you now drive trying
not to notice
the clearing sky.

You wish your bed were already
warm, your pillow
damp with the tears

you know she will give you,
her only friend
like rain

so rare
under the stars
and the clearing sky.

Revealing Oneself to a Woman

The creaking of the universe must be, for those
large enough, slow enough to vibrate to its tune,
must be like what I heard on the river
when I lay waiting for sleep and the barge
we lived on listed and each separate plank
spoke and the lashings and moorings pulled
from the touch of slow water,
burned a wide sound to the bone.

Sometimes in the night I see
the flesh as flame circling the bone. Slow.
Surely it is to light my way into Orion to live
for the next one thousand years.

The birds, too, are blaze of flesh flying:
I hear them at night. Voices
dark and shrill as air, blue,
shine and cast bright shadows on the wall;

                              the dry house
catches and goes like the rug before the fire
from the spark of their song.

There is no defense in the night
but to catch flame and go
large-wheeling at the dance.
We shall die in the light of our making.

The Fundamentalist

The morning washed once more
after a flood of dream.
A spotted sun
or a flock of starlings
or the Russian Air Force
shot down on the DEW Line:

God has a tin ear
large as any radar dish.
The Bible is his only home,
he is not a religious man,
he doesn't know he lives there.
Floods and nagging wives
and too many children at once
trying to get to the bathroom,
these things will touch
the best of us.

His name is not really God,
but he is blond. Once
he knew the light of sun
intimately; he lay on white
rocks without pain, he watched
goats graze on tiny blue flowers.
His daughters did the work—
he was a philosopher of sorts.

He never dials the last digit
of any phone number,
no one ever answers.
The earth will wash clean anyway
like a white shirt on the line
every morning.

The Astronomer Works Nights:
A Parable of Science

Lobachevsky . . . and Bolyai . . . first asserted
and proved that the axiom of parallels is
not necessarily true.
—*H. P. Manning*

Opusculum paedagogum. | The pears are not viols
—*Wallace Stevens*

What else in this dark world turns true?
Three pears and an apple in the bowl
on my table near the charts, dust,
the memory of silver stars, and breakfast.
Stars pop

like corn on a griddle if you watch them
as I do. The greatest calamities
the universe has known make no sound
like the deadliest trees in the forest.
Stars leave eggs under the fingernails
while you sleep.

I look at points and I make lines
to link stars in sleep which comes
with the sun. I have never touched
what alone I love, which is the light
which is clean and cold
as I am.

My wife and daughter loved me before
my skin grew translucent as a lampshade;
I can see stars through it when I hold
my hand against the night.

What I *do* is photograph
a section of the sky
smaller than the last
segment of the orange
after you took a bite.
Then I measure
the negatives.

While a student twenty
years ago I walked
the wet brick paths
on cooling afternoons;
I listened to the sky
crack as heat escaped;
I would not eat for days
because I liked
the strange dark feeling
(or sometimes half
an orange, closely peeled).

☆

The bones glow white as stars
hidden in the map of flesh
and the universe laughs quietly
just over some dark ridge.

Perhaps I *can* hear it
ticking like an engine block
cooling on the side of the road
while adulterers walk
arm in arm in the woods.

Slow Hercules stalks Cygnus
and the Dragon insinuates between:
some nights I see it all come true;

I am the cosmic peeping Tom,
and what intimacies I spy on
through stars like wistful windows
while beauty lies sadly
with the world.

But when I wander home and hear
a wife and lover laughing in the shadows
I wonder whether some night I might watch
a dance much closer if not more slow;

our final hope is that we will not know.

Martyrdom: A Love Poem

Each of the dozen Saints is bound
to his own stake, so like a prize
tomato. We know each death
will bear a flame red fruit.

When necessity lugs us into another year
do not be misled by calendars, a new year
begins with each tick, each time you
remember time is passing. And what a pet
you've made with a numbered dial
around time's neck, a leash
of pendulum to walk it
once around the block before you sleep.
At night time gathers itself,
a pack of neighborhood dogs
to knock over your garbage cans
to gnaw your discarded secrets
scattered for the neighbors to see if they,
bothered by the noise, will look
at your small life withering
in the dew of the backyard grass.

You and I owe nothing to sanctity,
find there no help at all, nothing
so dangerous makes us what martyrs are—
we have visions of each other
in our sleep, we know the secrets,
we have touched each other's
intimate places. We love because
it grows late and the tomatoes
are ripening. A morning glory

climbs one stake, mingles with the crude
green-and-pink-striped fruit: tomorrow
we will look at what we've done.

Certainly I would die for you:
that is the easy part, like falling
from grace or off a log.

III

He slew them at surprising distances
  with his gun.
Over a body held in his hand,
  his head was bowed low,
But not in grief.

                    —*Robert Penn Warren*

Mourning His Mother's Death

for Carolyn Kizer

We are all young wives once each winter, wish cold
snow into petals, see blood on the thorn.
The world cannot wait much longer
for a race of new wives to sweep the snow,
to prune dry branches in the hope of color.

This young mother dies of a secret cancer
at home in Tennessee. There is pain in my womb
and children can kill.

Late at night snow covers the tracks of small animals:
we grow smaller in the dark
until our rooms lose us in corners
and our mothers' slippered feet
move farther down the hall.

We stand by fire in the morning,
we dress slowly and look
at the snow for signs of life.

To Bury a Horse in Texas

Thirty years old, the only horse
we owned died on Christmas Eve:
my mother saw the feet flashing
in the winter light
trying to touch ground. She cried.
Father shot three times,
did not know the spot so somewhere
between the eyes it
took the hint, gave up.

What do you do with a horse dead
for Christmas, the renderers closed
till New Year, flies catching the scent?
You and all your brothers dig
while the sun shines, you watch
its side where a last breath
gathers through the day.

The yellow earth opened beside it.
We dug close to drag it less far.
We covered it. For Christmas
that year I got boots and guns
to play at cowboy.

In the white night a horse floats in awful
phosphorescence. The mad child rides
brandishing silver guns with the message
in red on the barrels: *Kill him for me,*
             I am so young.

An Old Woman Walks Home

Done, and I am better for it, in the park I did dance
long and hard in the dark. Whoever saw did not care
and the small bare circle left in the grass could be
where the children stamped home plate, or where the gardener
missed last spring with his cans and powders. A dance
or two in the summer, discreetly small, cannot hurt me

like carnations can, or the colors of fall invading
the tips of the bougainvillea. I was a young dancer
fifty winters ago, but that is not my loss.
I can count the red carnations on my way home
and I think of children dead and rich and gone.
Oh we all suffer losses like the dance. Like faith

or a limber leg or the smell of last night's fish
in the morning. There is no story to my future but my past
is warm and rancid. I shall count the blood red flowers
in the night like stars. A vague wind comes
to cool my face but my feet hurt. That, you remember,
was always my problem. You remember me now.

With Hidden Noise

there is no solution
because there is no problem
—*Marcel Duchamp*

He walks with his daughters along a beach.

"Puberty" he tells them "is like a box,
is mysterious only if closed."
He tells them because
he has always opened boxes:
his ambiguous trail lies littered with ribbons
and tissue and addresses on the wrappers ripped
in two. They can be read
but it does not matter, he lives there.

"It is written like a diary" he says
"and is private and grammatically wrong.
That is a reason for locks."

                    Waves
flick edges of foam into his vision
but it does not matter because
he does not look.

He allows his daughters five minutes to swim.
They shiver in his sight;
he gazes at them open,
strewing the waves with themselves.
He hears a single syllable; they cry
because the water is cold.

Poems for a Tall, Sad Lady

1. A Place to Begin

To begin somewhere, during a red afternoon
she would lean on an elbow and write letters
on a polished desk
dark as her lacquered nails.

She would write letters home to a mother or two,
once or twice to a father,
a brother, an imaginary lover,
on a red, or reddish, afternoon.

2. Hunger

In Vienna there is a small house with blue shutters
under the evening shadow of a Lutheran church.
In the house you may be served a dish
named for a saint: *Gateau Saint-Honoré.*
It is made of dozens of eggs, spun sugar,
pâte sucrée, crème chantilly.
Served with coffee, black.

She was never in Vienna.

Such sweet disappointments and hunger
make her thin and round-eyed.

3. Romance

In Katmandu she stopped in the street
to shut her eyes to the sound of men and boys.
Someone put a hand to her chest:
perhaps it was her own left hand,
her eyes were closed, she didn't know.

She walked round-eyed again and bought small bells
in red shops. She rang her way home on ship
and listened to stories of pirates
who cut the sullen waves and flesh
with sharp-edged ships and knives.

4. Being Lonely

Being in bed with a man for the first time
at age thirty-one, she watched the fire grow dim, late, and quiet.
His head stirred heavily against her bruised right thigh
as she talked: she told him about the morgue in Boston,
how she saw a burned body,
a man with arms crossed over his head where timbers fell,
and the body brown as an old saddle full of the smell of horse.

As the light washed in the windows
she said it was preparation for men, why she went;
and a way to know the look of bodies without a mirror.
She said to a sleeping man it was only
something to do
one warm red afternoon.

5. Secrets in Her Life

The order of things is surely this:
red next to yellow, a bracelet
she will not wear
but will not throw away,

a box with a strong brass lock.

6. Occasional Endings

Along a glittering path under the small bridges
beside a lake where people pretend, for hours, she walks.

Her life is full of such beginnings:
she wears green on Tuesdays, and a large maroon-colored ring,
soft sheened, which she turns
and turns on her finger till it cuts.
Then she stops. And begins again.

7. Posterity

We all have children. Hers
are of infinite ages. She watches them
visit the zoo—hordes descend on the lion,
the giraffe, the flimsy elephant
with the suppurating leg.

She buys them popcorn and they forget
to say thank you. They are concerned
for the small monkeys
which seem to be dead.

Picnic on the Beach

Small season, a warm day, consolation for a hard winter
and a time to commit small crimes. Like killing each other,
or slashing the cabbage heads cold from the ice,
or spying on ourselves through mirrors
dirty as the scales of fish on the beach which do not shine
under the winter sun:

my daughter on the beach whirls
in sympathy with gulls. If I listen
long enough to this pink shell
I will hear her speak to me again.
She will say *You were right, Father,*
it was all my fault. I should never have grown
this round in the breast, this tall—
I shall never do it again.

Then I would walk home holding her,
then I would touch the dangerous spots she wears,
I would teach her the slippery edge
of men like me.

My daughter is angry with me while I eat cabbage
on the beach. The gulls are carnivorous as daughters,
they leave me alone with my salad.

On the Whiteness of the Whale: Discovery

                      Lost. Never
found what we came for:
                        expeditions into snow
are never taken as seriously
as sex with a sly wife
or riding a horse through the Argentine.

The stars are unreliable
and the earth moves out from beneath us.

What is not white on the inside?
If I cut my hand on this page
the bloodless flesh is white
and sweet as the core of an apple;
inside the seed is bright
as white pigeons circling like love.
From inside a drift in Antarctica
Amundsen extends a greeting
(he has awaited this moment,
his bride, since 1928):

It was all a joke. Who would leave home
forever to find the cold bottom
of this earth? The pole
was not worth it.

The grass in Norway turns white under the moon
while barns blaze into diamond.
The horses of the night
run slowly through their own frozen vapor.

The Good Wife's Cooking

Learned, less necessary than sex
or language,
but of great convenience
during long afternoons
filled with soft touchings.

She beheads fish quickly,
succinctly—the cat chews
both eyes of the flounder,
the bones unzip themselves,
the onions brown to her song.

Lying in her cold mouth
at night,
her life remains
hidden and raw.

The Jays

        descend,
hordes ringing
like bells from a cold sky
this cold morning
of a gray day.
Sounding brass and tinkling,
they speak
in tongues; I have heard
the voice of blue jays at the oddest
moments of my life, like birth
perhaps, or that morning
like this when I awoke
in that strange machine,
my grandfather's bed.
The woods rang
shamelessly, their infinite
music harsher than the cold
floor where I stood
to watch them
harass the cows.
I have not been back to his farm
where he and his ringing world
died twelve years ago.
I live in a sort of city,
a place where a few fat birds,
a jay or two, hesitant,
speak to us from the wires,
say nothing of significance,
say it is over, childhood,
innocence, whatever
lies we once said we knew.
If you walk quietly

late at night, sometimes
your casual foot will raise one—
you will stand listening
to an old voice,
cold comfort, a lie.
Then you return to bed
to dream that it is morning,
that blue jays sing for joy alone,
that they, like you,
have nothing much to say.

Anniversary Waltz

Each spring we dance
as if we're hollow boned
no good for walking
on two feet, hands for flying.

We have known each other too long
to take this seriously.
We are married in mind
which is to say we are tired,

but this one night we dance
and someone plays
a tight small trumpet
like he knows us

and wishes us better
than we wish ourselves.

The Green Horse

Who could be smaller than this child
on the four-horse carousel which plays
the Washington Post March
in front of the discount store?
He cares. His father
counts the time lost more than the quarter.

The child refuses distraction.
He holds tightly and watches
the neck of the yellow horse
while riding the red
in a kind of kept time.

We remember wanting to ride
in front of the supermarkets,
we all look at the child
for an embarrassed moment before
pushing the revolving door. We look
to see if he is there when we come out again.

He cannot be there. No father
will put more than two quarters in,
too much pain. I have never seen
more than two children at one time
on a four-horse carousel. I have never seen

the money removed.
What would it be like to see someone
across the room at a party,
to call out "We met once
twenty years ago,
in front of K-Mart, I was on
the blue horse, you were on the green." To call out.

Paul Verlaine at the Grave of Lucien Létinois

. . . his grave was conceded to him for ten years. The concession was not renewed, and presumably his bones were then thrown away.
—*Joanna Richardson*, Verlaine

What does the world with its lung of ocean breathe
if not our pale and fetid dust? We have friends
and we love more than is good for us. A decade
is time enough to forget the other things we did:
a small attempt at murder—amateurish, *mon amour*—
revives the mind admirably . . .

that was the other one, my Arthur. But if you
were not my *grand* passion you were my best. The loss
of money meant the loss of your sweet bones
—you do forgive me—while his I still wear
red and clotted in my skin. I
am too ugly to grieve this way:

this picture is not pretty beneath the trees
beside the wound of earth, reopened, the grave
of someone no longer you. You knew my wounds
and wore them well.

I can, Lucien, still write:
that would please you. I recite for dinners
and for drinks. Mainly for drinks. The century wears
to a ragged close. They will forgive you,
they will forget you—your dust ultimately dissolved—
as they should.
They will watch my grave
over their left shoulders;
they will read my poems
like gambling debts, thinking:

they are pretty now;
that face is gone;
and when his only friend
died young,
he could not buy his bones.

The Last of the Love Poems

for Ivan Nagy

On a gray edge three figures feed swans;
a man on a balcony overlooks the lake,
picks at his feet which bleed. Rich
with itself the world accepts
our only embrace indifferently.
We submit to its skin
like peaches, cold in silver bowls.

I watched you dance, you dancing;
my ladies come and go, they are
shadows on the wall. Across
the street there are couples
throwing bread to the swans
which pick out only the soft parts.

The proper word would save me,
could populate whole nations
I dream of in my bed. I will kiss
you if you ask:
your mouth would grow large
in the dark, and silent.

People in this world trust
only words, silence
is our only alarm:
for a delicate hour
you danced in darkness:

a small phrase from you
and your daughter is safe.
You could end my prowling
your streets; I will sleep
with you if you wish,
but that will not keep me away.

If you ask me to dance
you may hold me;
you may feed me grapes
if you peel them.

*Come, let us be bored
together:* my dear,
we are hunters at dance,
the prize is *always* bloodied:

I sit with my feet in my hands;
there are shadows in the house,
the bed cools through the day
far from swans and the sun.
I shall eat only the soft parts
like love, like small dancing.

IV

*It would be doing them an injustice
to think that they wanted to seduce;
they knew they had claws and sterile
wombs, and they lamented this aloud.
They could not help it if their laments
sounded so beautiful.*

—*Franz Kafka*

Infidelity

He was a man married in mind and body
in all the best ways. He wrote letters to a lover
while his wife slept. He was a man who enjoyed
his guilt like old wine, who said *love* with passion
and meant it. He lived well in a small room.

Once he rode through Mexico on a spotted horse
and wore spurs, and for days at a time would dream;
once he visited Guevara in the green jungle,
ate roasted parrot and smiled.

He particularly enjoys short women
with large breasts. He watches them walk
and he gives them names, families, fathers
whom he went to war with, and pets
with long gold-tipped hair.

Whatever a man thinks about dying he denies
even though he will say it. His afflicted
sleep is all the day leaves him
after the ravages of its happiness.

So at night he writes letters to a lover
while his wife sleeps
in their dark and dangerous bed.
The sun rises over Moscow while he licks
the sharp edge of the envelope. Once
he cut his tongue so deeply he cried.

The Husband's Guilt

The cult perished.
The empty city welcomed the monkeys.
—John Berryman

1

See the ripple in the woman. One or two
out of place curves we glide over and wives
still wait out the angry evenings.
Messages slip within the body:
adultery is a paltry sin, not worth writing
home about. But then, home crumbles,
no city welcomes me, calls me
New Balboa, Cartographer of Fleshy Coasts
Who Tastes the New Exotik and dips himself—
his dismal nakedness—into Fountains
of sullen Youth. Adultery is a paltry sin:
I hurried to the ruin. The old city echoed
faint small footsteps. Taking small
pieces of Greece while the guide wasn't looking,
I toured the Parthenon. Small marble
in the pocket, something touched by Praxiteles,
perhaps, or anyone anonymous three thousand
years ago. Home again I found arrowheads
and shards in the banks of the bayous:
again the feeling, the heat starts deep in the bone.

2

My wife spins wool by hand, her two smooth
strong hands move like years.
She does it because she wants to, has nothing
planned for the thread, yards of yarn
piled round her knees. Has no plans.
The fingers grew strong tapping out stories
telling of home, of children, of her mariner

husband. She now sits alone. She makes
the old memories of women who waited,
who spun their only gold from urine-wet wool;
of women who waited for men who had
nothing to do in the long night either.

Biography of a Strangler

His own daughter died in his hands
one day while the wife and son laughed
on the beach; the color of sand
blinded him and he cried for a moment.

He learned many things after that:
his sons went off to school,
the wife had other daughters, other lovers.
No one could ask for more.

The time was right for war.
For all daughters dead in the hand
he fought the Germans. For all
daughters dead

he fought the Japanese. For
all the dead daughters of all
the sweaty palms, he fought
the Russians: since nothing

comes home alive from the dark wood
of Europe, you cannot choose
whom you love. This is the story
of one man's long life.

What It Might Mean to Be Alive

Learn nothing from it, but listen to dreams
escape when the edge of the sky grays
and the bedroom phosphoresces; listen
to a habit of middle age. Watch the car
slam sideways into the tree; hear
familiar flesh tear, and be alone again.

Why do I dream that my wife dies in a car wreck?
Because the light weakens and I stare again
at the shadow beside me. Or because knowledge
of woman's flesh demands pain, like a tooth jerked
out roughly that the dentist shows you:

he smiles and says it's your own fault;
if you grew hair all over your body and grazed
like an animal or a king from the Bible
your teeth would be perfect. I called her perfect
when we went to bed, and we cried together,
telling each other we cried for joy.

My teeth hurt this morning. I imagine
how her mouth feels crunched against the wheel—
I hope it ends quickly.

A girl I know will comfort me in my loss.
She is young: when she smiles
a white light leaps from her teeth.
I have never seen anyone
lovely as this light.
I pretend I am alive. I touch the light.

The Movements of Birds like Years

He saw brightly through the trees
a barn of cypress the morning he was twelve years old.
A crane whiter than possible in that angle of the sun
flew slower than history past the gray,
feathery planks. A barn beyond imagining, forbidden.

In twenty years nothing shone brighter, not women
nor the taste of the blade's edge in the mouth,
the sharp taste of steel which cuts saliva.
He hunted a little through the day,

he walked in circles, he shot
once. He felt the barn grow precious
in its light like a blister. He touched it
with his tongue.

He saw the last crane
fly to the nest that night, its feathers blue from the sun
going. He entered the high barn and knelt
behind bales of hay clean and full of themselves

he took himself in his hands
and watched pale women he could never know; imagined
blond ones in the loft, a choir watching. Not enough,
but something to block for a moment the light;

his hand trembled when he finished. His own smell sharper
than the hay pushed him up the path home
but he turned once and looked at the barn in last light
as if women were there, waiting till he grew
a few more years.

                                  Twenty years is enough
to destroy an abandoned barn. And the death

                                 of a large white bird
in the shaft of sun through the trees makes him lonely.
So does the lock on his daughter's diary
opened with a hair-pin.

Anger, Adolescence, and Menarche

for my sister

I have nothing to show for it, no seared
image of lust in the garden under the forsythia,
no lost nights in the desert
pregnant with stars, lizards, rocks.

To the beach, years ago, we raced
past fish shining on sand, some dead,
some patiently alive waiting for the wave
which will, as we thought then,
recover them, forgive dalliance
at the edges: I forgive you
everything

except that we had no plum trees
to sit under during afternoons to watch
the light shift slightly, slowly through an hour;
where there should be silver bowls on white
wicker benches and we should not eat
plums from the tree but only those
carried out cold from the kitchen
with drops like new eyes on their skins:

whatever unfolded from you like fire
I did not see. It lit up your long night
which was childhood—you have
a child of your own, yet I see you
smaller than any living mother,
I see you standing in your flannel gown asking
if we *have* to love our mother.

I left you and you became
only yourself. Yet I do believe you.
You love yourself too little, too carefully:
you still believe in sin.

Sometimes the answer is easy: Yes,
I loved her, but you are still alive;
try to be good and write to me
when you are grown and I am rich.
Try to be better. What else can I forgive you?
Ask me anything. Hand me the last plum,
or eat it yourself.

Appalling Light

for Catherine Iino

1

We live in a cruel country; hope
savages the century. Alone on a hill
overlooking the smoking ruins
a quiet ghost bides his time.

What I remember most clearly is
a white butterfly—a sulphur—
skimming, briefly touching
the softly heaped garbage.

2

White, white, white, white:
under lights pale
men wave
limp hands as if
that prodigious energy,
beauty, were an illness.

As we turn the corner
you touch my arm as if
to ask: "You
don't know them, do you?"

3

The last bride of the day walks
on strewn camellias. It has been
a long day. The priest mutters
but she will not be hurried,
it can never happen again,
this efflorescence of sex
in public. What the ushers whisper
in the glass-stained light
must be true, and yet her veil
floats like light shimmering
among feldspar pebbles in the stream
five miles into the mountains.

Confessio Amantis:
For Frederick Rolfe, Baron Corvo

. . . earned no fame and deserved
few friends. . . .
—Shane Leslie, introduction to
A History of the Borgias

And gets no sympathy from me, this man
who wrote in heliotrope ink, disguised
himself in wig and painted face avoiding
creditors, such a man can be
all bad. We are all
proud of our vices, and let the virtues go.

I designed furniture and fire irons,
I delineated saints and seraphim
and sinners, a series of rather interesting
and polyonymous devils in a period
of desperate revolt.

And he was once a photographer. Picture it,
this peculiar man standing at the box,
he tells you Be still, look a little
to the right. Be still, damn it.

He wanted to be a priest. They kicked him
out, so he told on them. Few of us
can so utterly resist growing up.

Anyway, when I was fourteen, a member
of the Passionist Order tried to get me
to join. He brought movies to my house,
the boys playing soccer, the lovely
light in the chapel, healthy faces beckoning,
beaconing, making a vice of virtue,
or vice versa—so unutterably young!

After the film we went alone into the kitchen,
my family waiting in the living room, mother
praying (I never knew what for). The priest
asked if I had anything to confess; I had,
but said no, would not tell him, a friend
of the family. Jerking off is a mortal sin.
He gave me Communion, my first major sacrilege.

☆

Surely you, too have a secret,
some trifle you would kill
for, to keep out of the papers.
Sometimes a hieroglyph of cloud
announces mine in the morning
splashed red by the sun.
Last week I saw a porno film:
in the dark fifteen of us prayed
that no one would turn around:
not one of us, I think, saw
whatever they did on the screen—
it is hard to look up
with averted eyes.

Anyway, back home we brothers,
though we lived in the country,
we had no sheep, only each other.
I was the youngest small sailor
(some say in the navy you need
a cork to get any sleep at night).

☆

Someone erased
my message
before I arrived;
this telephone has two
mouthpieces.
I speak but

like praying
I am my only
answer.
Oh, it is hard,
dreadful, to be
in love. I read
magazines
in the bus station
in Indianapolis.

The beautiful young men walk
quickly as chickens back
and forth in front of me.
They carry canes and wear feathers.
All of this, and love,
at four o'clock in the morning.

A man could live in Indianapolis
if he never left the station.
Intrigue, an aroma
of travel, and rhythmic
nights, what more
could a man want
than to be wanted
at four a.m.

They love
each other, those two
who cross under the brilliant
lights which could make cacti
bloom in a bus station
even this time of the morning.

It is a little like life,
the way I sigh: my bus
is announced, I must continue
to Chicago. Nothing remains
and young men will soon be old

without me. You cannot choose
whom you love
on the way to Chicago.